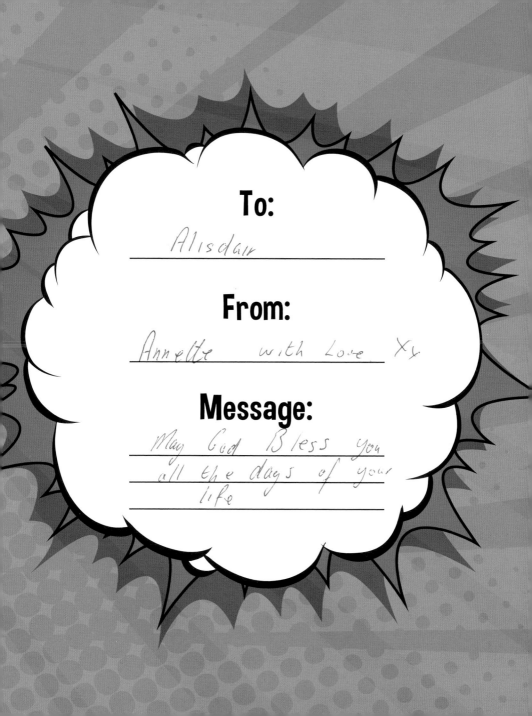

Super Heroes Devotional

Copyright © 2016 by Christian Art Kids,
an imprint of Christian Art Publishers,
PO Box 1599, Vereeniging, 1930, RSA

359 Longview Drive, Bloomingdale, IL, 60108, USA

First edition 2016

Designed by Christian Art Kids

Illustrations by Joe Goode

Images used under license from Shutterstock.com

Scripture quotations are taken from the *Holy Bible,* New Living Translation®,
copyright © 1996, 2004, 2007, 2013 by Tyndale House Foundation.
Used by permission of Tyndale House Publishers, Inc., Carol Stream,
Illinois 60188. All rights reserved.

Set in 13 on 14pt Clearwater by Christian Art Kids

Printed in China

ISBN 978-1-4321-1426-8

16 17 18 19 20 21 22 23 24 25 – 10 9 8 7 6 5 4 3 2 1

SUPER HEROES DEVOTIONAL

WRITTEN BY CAROLYN LARSEN
ILLUSTRATED BY JOE GOODE

christian art kids

Contents

1

God Is Most Important

"If you love Me, obey My commandments."
— JOHN 14:15 —

Nothing should be more important to you than God.

- Not friends.
- Not video games.
- Not sports.
- Nothing.

It's OK to like those things, but how do you make sure God is most important?

Spend time with Him by reading the Bible. Talk to Him in prayer. Think about how He would want you to behave.

Remember:
A Super Hero ... does not let anything be more important than God.

2

Respecting God's Name

"You must not misuse the name of the LORD your God."
— EXODUS 20:7 —

Respect for God shows in your actions and in what you say. Some people use God's name as an expression of frustration or anger.

They may even use it when they are happy or surprised. God's name should not be used in that way. His name is special because He is special.

Remember:
A Super Hero ... does not use God's name in a bad way.

3

God's Day Is Special

"Remember to observe the Sabbath day by keeping it holy."
— EXODUS 20:8 —

Some celebrate God's day on Saturday. Some observe it on Sunday. Whichever day your family chooses, God's day should be honored.

How?

Some do not allow any work to be done on God's day. It's a day for worship and prayer. Others do some normal things, but first go to church. They make time that day to think about God. They make God's day different from a normal day to honor Him.

Remember:
A Super Hero … makes God's day special.

Treating Parents with Respect

4

"Honor your father and mother."
— EXODUS 20:12 —

You honor your parents when you respect them.

Respect for them is shown by how you speak to them. You should not talk back when they tell you to do something. You should not whine about things. A respectful child doesn't argue with his parents.

Respect means obeying parents' rules because you understand their rules are there to protect you and help you learn to be a good person.

Respect is important.

Remember:
A Super Hero ... respects his parents.

Thinking about Other People

Be kind to each other, tenderhearted, forgiving one another,
just as God through Christ has forgiven you.
— EPHESIANS 4:32 —

Are you always kind? If you are playing nicely with your friend, you are probably kind. But, what if he wrecks your game or wants to play something else? Or, what if he is mean to you? Are you nice anyway?

It's not an easy thing to do, but God's Super Hero is kind to others — no matter what — because that is what God says to do.

Remember:
A Super Hero ... is kind to others.

Don't Take Things That Aren't Yours

"You must not steal."
— EXODUS 20:15 —

Remember:
A Super Hero ...
does not steal.

Your parents have probably told you this many times: "Don't take things that do not belong to you."

Even if your friend has something you really, really want. Even if no one would know that you took it. (God always knows.)

Why?

God says it is wrong to take something that doesn't belong to you. How would you feel if your friend took something from you without asking? If you want it, work for it. Save for it. Don't take what someone else has.

13

7

Honesty Is Best

Don't lie to each other.
— COLOSSIANS 3:9 —

"Mommy, I didn't knock the lamp over. It fell all by itself."
"No, I didn't hit Tommy, my hand accidentally landed on his head ... hard." These are examples of NOT telling the truth.

Do you try to protect yourself by changing the story just a little or maybe by telling PART of the truth?

A Super Hero doesn't do that because it is lying. God says to tell the truth and take whatever comes because of it.

Remember:
A Super Hero ... tells the truth.

Try and Try Again

Lazy people want much but get little, but those who work hard will prosper.
— PROVERBS 13:4 —

Learning something new takes work. But, once you've learned things like how to ride a bike, do math, spell, or master a level on your video game, then you've learned it! What's the key to learning something new? Keep trying over and over.

Ask someone who knows how to do it if they will help you. Ask God to help you pay attention to what you need to learn.

Remember:
A Super Hero ... doesn't give up.

9

Asking God for Help

Never stop praying.
— 1 THESSALONIANS 5:17 —

Your Super Hero power and strength come from God. So ... when you need to be strong or brave, ask God to help you.

When you need to be quiet and calm, ask His help.
Tell God what you're scared of.
Tell Him what you're excited about.
Tell Him what you're looking forward to.
 You can even tell Him what you don't want to do.

 You can tell God anything! Talking to God is
 called praying.

Remember:
A Super Hero ... talks to God.

Understanding Forgiveness

> If we confess our sins to Him, He is faithful and just to forgive us our sins and to cleanse us from all wickedness.
>
> — 1 JOHN 1:9 —

The Bible teaches, "Do this" or "Don't do that." Can anyone keep all of its rules?

Nope. Breaking God's rules is called sin and everyone is a sinner.

So, what happens then? Just the best thing ever! You tell God you are sorry (and mean it) and HE FORGIVES YOU! God is the Super Hero of forgiveness!

Remember:
A Super Hero ... knows he is forgiven.

11

Saying Thanks out Loud

Always be thankful.
— COLOSSIANS 3:15 —

Your parents take you on a great vacation. Your friend plays what you want to play. You get a gift that you really wanted.

How do these things make you feel? Happy? Excited? How about thankful? Sure, you probably feel thankful for the good time you had or the good things you received.

Did you tell the people who did these nice things that you're thankful?

It's important to say, "Thanks." Let others know you appreciate what they do for you.

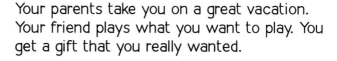

Remember:
A Super Hero ... is thankful.

Leading by Example

Be an example to all believers in what you say, in the way you live, in your love, your faith, and your purity.
— 1 TIMOTHY 4:12 —

Remember:
A Super Hero ...
is a good leader.

If others do what you want, you are a leader. That's a big responsibility. You can lead in good ways or bad ways.

You can lead others to:
- be kind.
- be honest.
- honor God.
- play by the rules
- be respectful.

Use your Super Hero power to show others how to be kind and fair. Most importantly, lead them to God by the example of how you live!

13

Learning New Things

Let us stop going over the basic teachings about Christ again and again.
Let us go on instead and become mature in our understanding.
— HEBREWS 6:1 —

The longer a Super Hero knows God, the more he learns about obeying Him and living the way God says to live.

You don't have to know everything now.
Learning goes on all your life, so:
Read the Bible. Learn from Sunday school and church. Learn from people who have known God a long time.

Remember:
A Super Hero ... learns new things.

No Fear

Be strong and courageous! Do not be afraid or discouraged.
For the LORD your God is with you wherever you go.
— JOSHUA 1:9 —

Some things are scary, aren't they? Do you always have to be brave or is it OK to be scared sometimes?

The truth is that no one is brave ALL the time.

But, when a Super Hero starts to feel scared, what does he do? He remembers that God is always with him. He remembers that God protects him. He remembers that God will help him be brave if he just asks for help.

Remember:
A Super Hero ... is brave.

15

What Did You Say?

Don't just listen to God's Word.
You must do what it says.
— JAMES 1:22 —

Are you a good listener? Before you say, "Sure," think about what that means ...

When Mom is telling you something, you pay attention and try to do what she says.

When your teacher is showing you how to add or subtract or how to spell a word, you listen and learn.

Most importantly, you listen to God by reading His Word and learning from it.

Listening is the best way to learn.

Remember:
A Super Hero ... listens.

Keep Working!

> Good planning and hard work lead to prosperity,
> but hasty shortcuts lead to poverty.
> — PROVERBS 21:5 —

Some things are hard work. School work may be hard. Some chores are hard. Learning a new skill in sports is hard.

What does a Super Hero do when something is hard? Does he try once or twice and then give up?

Of course not! A Super Hero works hard to learn new things. He wants to get better and better at them. Why? Because he wants to be the best Super Hero he can be!

Remember:
A Super Hero ... works hard.

Telling Others

"Go and make disciples of all the nations."
— MATTHEW 28:19 —

Do you love to talk about your favorite thing? Maybe you have a favorite video game or maybe there is an athlete you admire a lot.

When there is something that you love, you probably talk about it to anyone who will listen!

Does Jesus fall into that category? Do you tell others about Him? Do your friends know that Jesus is important to you? Have you found a way to share His love with others?

Remember:
A Super Hero ... shares Jesus' love.

Making Good Choices

Your word is a lamp to guide my feet and a light for my path.
— PSALM 119:105 —

Every day you make choices. You choose to obey or disobey. You choose to be kind or unkind. You choose to speak nice words or angry words. You choose to be respectful or disrespectful.

A Super Hero who wants to show his love for God chooses to obey God and obey his parents. He is kind and is nice to others.

The way to make wise choices is to know what the Bible says. Learn how God wants you to live.

19

God Made Me!

God opposes the proud but gives grace to the humble.
— JAMES 4:6 —

What does "humble" mean? It means not bragging about how great you are, but instead cheering for someone else — and meaning it! It's no fun to be around someone who only cheers for himself, isn't it?

A Super Hero knows that his strength, his talents and his skills are all gifts from God ... so he has nothing to brag about. That means he can cheer for others and thank God for all his abilities.

Remember:
A Super Hero ... is humble.

Obedience Rules!

Children, obey your parents because you belong
to the Lord, for this is the right thing to do.
— EPHESIANS 6:1 —

Parents have rules. But, they don't make rules just for fun or insist that you obey because they have nothing better to do.

- Rules keep you safe from danger.
- Rules help you to learn to be a better person.
- Rules help you to get along with others.
- Rules teach you to respect God, parents, teachers and the law.

Obeying your parents helps you become a better Super Hero!

Remember:
A Super Hero ... obeys his parents.

27

A Super Helper!

Two people are better off than one,
for they can help each other succeed.
— ECCLESIASTES 4:9 —

Playing is fun. Hanging out with friends is fun. Helping can be fun too. Helping others shows that you care about them.

A Super Hero is always a helper! How can you be a helper?

Carry a basket of laundry upstairs for Mom. Empty the dishwasher. Put your toys away. Play with your younger brother or sister. Help Dad in the garden.

Show God's love to others by being a helper.

Remember:
A Super Hero ... helps others.

Say You're Sorry and Mean It!

> I confessed all my sins to You and stopped trying to hide my guilt ... And You forgave me! All my guilt is gone.
>
> — PSALM 32:5 —

The Bible says that everyone sins. It also says that God will forgive your sin.

Ask God to forgive your sins. But ... mean it. Don't think you can do whatever you want, then run to God and mumble, "Forgive me."

Be honestly sorry and ask for His help to never do that thing again. When you are tempted, ask God for strength to help you resist.

Remember:
A Super Hero ... asks for forgiveness.

23

When Things Are Scary

Trust in the LORD with all your heart;
do not depend on your own understanding.
— PROVERBS 3:5 —

God says that He loves you. He will always be there for you. Can you believe Him when scary things happen? Things like your family moving away from everyone you know? Or when someone you love gets really sick?

Do you trust God to help you through these things?

It's OK to be scared sometimes, but remember God's promise ... and trust Him to keep His word.

Remember:
A Super Hero ... trusts God.

Playing Fair

Honesty guides good people; dishonesty
destroys treacherous people.
— PROVERBS 11:3 —

Remember:
A Super Hero ...
plays by the
rules.

Do you want to win so much that you ignore the
real rules of a game and make up your own
rules just to make sure you win? That's
cheating. It isn't fair to friends who play
games with you.

A Super Hero plays by the rules
because that's the fair thing to do.
It shows respect for God's rules
and ... sometimes even a Super
Hero has to learn how to lose.

We can't be good at everything
and sometimes we do have to
lose.

Sharing What You Have

All the believers were united in heart and mind. And they felt that what they owned was not their own, so they shared everything they had.

— ACTS 4:32 —

You just got something awesome — a new toy or something. A friend comes over and just wants to try out your new toy. Do you share it or not? That's a hard one, isn't it?

Sometimes sharing isn't easy. Sometimes you just don't want to. Sharing shows that you care about your friend. It's the Super Hero thing to do!

Remember:
A Super Hero ... shares with others.

Doing What's Right

The LORD gives power to the weak and strength to the powerless.
— ISAIAH 40:29 —

It will happen someday if it hasn't already. A friend will try to get you to do something that you know you shouldn't do – something your parents have told you not to do. He might say, "No one will know." But someone will ... God ... and you.

A Super Hero stays strong and does what he knows is right. He asks God for strength to fight the temptation to do wrong.

Remember:
A Super Hero ... does what's right.

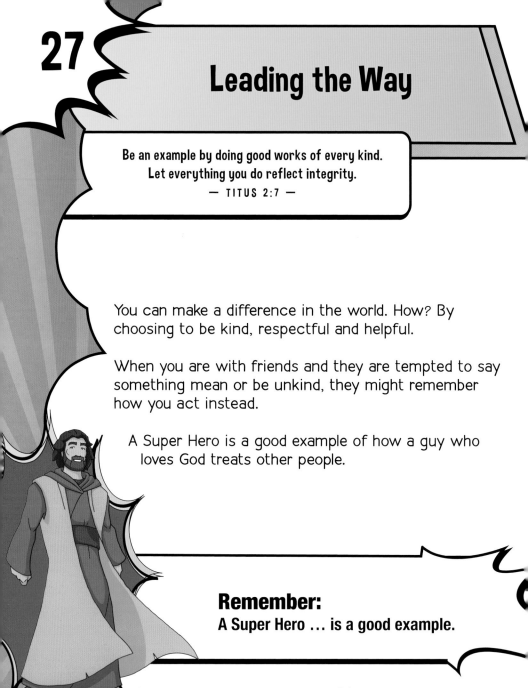

27

Leading the Way

Be an example by doing good works of every kind.
Let everything you do reflect integrity.
— TITUS 2:7 —

You can make a difference in the world. How? By choosing to be kind, respectful and helpful.

When you are with friends and they are tempted to say something mean or be unkind, they might remember how you act instead.

A Super Hero is a good example of how a guy who loves God treats other people.

Remember:
A Super Hero ... is a good example.

Taking the First Step

> "This is how God loved the world: He gave His one and only Son, so that everyone who believes in Him will not perish but have eternal life."
>
> — JOHN 3:16 —

Your parents take you to church. They read Bible stories to you. They teach you to pray before meals and before you go to sleep.

Those are good things — the first steps to knowing God. But, the next step is up to you. The beginning of your own life with God is believing that Jesus died for you.

You can learn more about Jesus by reading all about Him in the Bible.

Remember:
A Super Hero ... learns about Jesus.

Be Careful, Little Mouth, What You Say

Let everything you say be good and helpful, so that your words will be an encouragement to those who hear them.
— EPHESIANS 4:29 —

Words. You speak words all the time. They are just words, right? WRONG. The words you say can:

- make others feel bad.
- hurt feelings.
- be lies about someone else.

Or they can:

- make others feel great.
- be encouraging.
- be true.

What kind of words do you speak? Do you say words that will help others or hurt them?

Remember:
A Super Hero ... watches what he says.

God's Guidebook for You

I have hidden Your word in my heart,
that I might not sin against You.
— PSALM 119:11 —

Remember:
A Super Hero ...
learns God's
Word.

As God's Super Hero, you want to learn how to live the way God wants you to live. That means you need to learn what He wants. How do you discover that?

God made it easy. He gave you the Bible. It has stories of people who followed God. It has instructions for how you can live for Him and how you should treat other people. Make time to read the Bible and to talk to God.

Good Buddies

A friend is always loyal, and a brother is born to help in time of need.
— PROVERBS 17:17 —

What do you love most about your friends? Is it that you have a lot of fun with them? Do you like making up games together?

You can trust a friend to look out for you. A friend will stand up for you when someone picks on you. A good buddy will defend you against lies.

Friends are a gift from God. Are you a good friend to others?

Remember:
A Super Hero ... is a good friend.

The Best Thing to Do

The earnest prayer of a righteous person has great power and produces wonderful results.

— JAMES 5:16 —

When someone is sick ... pray for him.
When your friend is moving away ... pray for him.
When your dad loses his job ... pray for him.
When your new friend doesn't know God ... pray for him.
When your buddy is worried about his parents divorcing ... pray for him.

The best thing you can do is ... pray.

Remember:
A Super Hero ... prays for others.

33

Blessing Others

Put into action the generosity that comes from
your faith as you understand and experience
all the good things we have in Christ.

— PHILEMON 1:6 —

Are you saving money to buy something special? While you're saving, have you thought about giving some money away?

Some people don't have food or a place to live. Some have lost everything they have because of a storm. They aren't saving for something "special"; they are just trying to live.

Could you share some of your money with them? It's the God-thing to do.

Remember:
A Super Hero ... gives generously.

Helping Out

"Do to others whatever you would like them to do to you."
— MATTHEW 7:12 —

How could you help others? Look around. Are there elderly neighbors nearby? Could they use help getting their trashcan to the curb? Or picking up branches in their yard after a storm?

Do you have younger brothers or sisters you could entertain while Mom and Dad get things done? Could you empty the dishwasher?

A Super Hero shows God's love to others by being a helper.

Remember:
A Super Hero ... does what he can to help.

Forgiving Others

Make allowance for each other's faults, and forgive anyone who offends you.
Remember, the Lord forgave you, so you must forgive others.
— COLOSSIANS 3:13 —

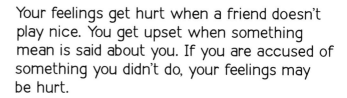

Your feelings get hurt when a friend doesn't play nice. You get upset when something mean is said about you. If you are accused of something you didn't do, your feelings may be hurt.

The best way to handle hurt is to forgive — that's the BEST way, but not the EASY way.

Remember that God forgives your sin. Others forgive you when you hurt them.

Remember:
A Super Hero ... forgives others.

Showing Courage

Be strong and courageous! The LORD your God will personally go ahead of you. He will neither fail you nor abandon you.
— DEUTERONOMY 31:6 —

Remember:
A Super Hero ...
is courageous
about new
things.

Some things are scary. For example, moving to a new town and starting a new school. All your friends are back in your old town and school.

It's OK to be a little afraid. New things are scary. What can you do? Ask God to help you. Remember He is always with you! Ask Him to help you be brave.

Have a positive attitude and trust God to bring new friends into your life.

Fighting Evil

Put on all of God's armor so that you will be able
to stand firm against all strategies of the devil.
— EPHESIANS 6:11 —

How can you fight evil?

Stick up for someone when others are telling lies about him.
Be friends with someone who has no friends.
Refuse to help friends damage someone else's property.
Pray for God to stop evil things that happen in the
world.

Will you be popular for fighting evil? Not
always, but it is the way to make a
difference in your world.

Remember:
A Super Hero ... fights evil.

No-Whine Zone

Sympathize with each other. Love each other as brothers
and sisters. Be tenderhearted, and keep a humble attitude.

— 1 PETER 3:8 —

When things don't go your way ... you want to whine.
When you get into trouble with your parents ... you want to whine.
When friends won't do what YOU want ... you want to whine.

Does whining make you feel better? Not
really. What's a better option? Have a
good attitude — an attitude like Jesus
would have — and move on!

Remember:
A Super Hero ... doesn't whine.

39 Taking Time for Thank You

Give thanks to the LORD, for He is good!
His faithful love endures forever.
— 1 CHRONICLES 16:34 —

Do you ask God for things when you pray? Things like healing someone who is sick or helping you with stuff? It's OK to pray for those things because God cares.

But do you remember to thank God too? Thank Him for your family, your home, your friends. Thank Him for Jesus and the Bible. Thank Him for answering your prayers, for forgiving your sin and for loving you.

Don't forget to thank God.

Remember:
A Super Hero ... remembers to thank God.

Real Worship

Great is the LORD! He is most worthy of praise!
— PSALM 96:4 —

What does it mean to worship God?
Does it mean paying attention in church?
Does it mean singing worship songs?
Does it mean memorizing Bible verses?

Those are all good things, but worship is something that grows out of your heart. Worship is your heart saying, "God, You are awesome, strong and powerful."

Worship means respecting God and making Him the most important person in your life. God is more important than friends, family, games, sports ... anything!

Remember:
A Super Hero ... worships God.

A God-Sized Celebration

I will exalt You, my God and King,
and praise Your name forever and ever.

— PSALM 145:1 —

When your favorite team wins, what do you do? You shout! You cheer! You celebrate! What do you do on your birthday? Have a party with your friends? Play games? Eat cake? Celebrate!!

When something special happens, most people celebrate. Do you ever think about celebrating God? Celebrate His love for you. Celebrate answers to your prayers. Celebrate how He takes care of you.

How about a big cheer for God? Yeah, a God-sized cheer!

Remember:
A Super Hero ... celebrates.

Fighting Temptation

When you are tempted, God will show you a way out so that you can endure.
— 1 CORINTHIANS 10:13 —

Remember:
A Super Hero ...
fights temptation.

Temptation is when you sort of want to do something you know is wrong. You know you shouldn't do it, but you can't stop thinking about it.

A Super Hero fights to keep that feeling away. How? When the thought to do that thing comes into your mind, you push it away. You think about something else. The best thing to do is to ask God to give you strength to fight temptation.

Then concentrate on something else, like doing your homework, tidying your room or hanging out with friends.

Calming Your Anger

Don't sin by letting anger control you.
— EPHESIANS 4:26 —

What happens when you get really mad? Do you yell? Do you hurt others? Do you break things? Are any of those good ways to handle anger?

Everyone gets angry sometimes. But, a Super Hero tries to control his anger. He tries not to hurt anyone or anything. He knows that losing his temper will only hurt others and make them upset with him. He asks God to help him be strong in controlling his anger.

Remember:
A Super Hero ... controls his anger.

Not by Yourself

"Be sure of this: I am with you always."
— MATTHEW 28:20 —

Grown-ups get busy with stuff. Friends sometimes choose to hang out with other friends. That can leave you feeling lonely.

Feeling like you're all alone can be a little scary. Even feeling like no one really understands what you're going through or what you're feeling is scary.

But, a Super Hero knows he is never really alone. God promises to be with him all the time ... forever!

Remember:
A Super Hero ... knows he is never alone.

Sticking like Glue!

As for me and my family, we will serve the LORD.
— JOSHUA 24:15 —

Do you have to think about obeying God every day? Yes. Start each day with a prayer asking God to help you stick close to Him. You can be sure that things will happen every day that try to pull you away from God.

Sometimes you have to CHOOSE to stick close to God instead of doing other things.

A Super Hero chooses to stick close to God, no matter what happens.

Remember:
A Super Hero ... sticks with God always!

No Jealousy

Anger is cruel, and wrath is like a flood,
but jealousy is even more dangerous.

— PROVERBS 27:4 —

Jealousy is what you feel when you really, really want something that someone else has. Or, you want to do what someone else gets to do.

Jealousy can cause problems between friends. It's hard to play nice with someone you're jealous of.

A Super Hero is thankful for what he has ... and for what his friends have.

Remember:
A Super Hero ... is not jealous.

47

I'm Good At ...

God has given us different gifts for doing certain things well.
— ROMANS 12:6 —

What are you good at? Everyone is good at something and whatever you are good at is God's gift to you.

Some people are good at sports. Some are good at music. Some are good at math. Some are good at being kind to others. Some are really good helpers.

Whatever you are good at — enjoy it! Enjoy doing it and enjoy that you're good at it. God wants you to enjoy the abilities He gave you!

Remember:
A Super Hero ... enjoys his abilities.

Nothing to Brag About

"Those who exalt themselves will be humbled,
and those who humble themselves will be exalted."
— MATTHEW 23:12 —

Remember:
A Super Hero ...
does not brag.

"Yay, me! I'm BETTER than the best!" That's what bragging sounds like. Guys who brag about stuff are not a lot of fun to be around. They don't pay much attention to what others are good at.

Wouldn't it be boring if we were all good at the same things?

A Super Hero doesn't brag about how good he is at something, because he knows that his abilities are a gift from God. So, he thanks God instead of bragging.

49

The Most Important Thing

You are all children of God through faith in Christ Jesus.
— GALATIANS 3:26 —

Things change. You get older. You change classes. You change teams. Friends change. People move away.

There are some things you can absolutely know for sure will never ever change. One of those is that you are God's child. He loves you. He watches out for you. He helps you. He teaches you.

A Super Hero knows that God is his father and he is God's child. That will never, ever change.

Remember:
A Super Hero ... knows he is God's child.

The Future

"I know the plans I have for you," says the LORD. "They are plans for good and not for disaster, to give you a future and a hope."
— JEREMIAH 29:11 —

God knows what's ahead for you. He has plans for your life. Things that happen to you teach you things you will need to know in the future. Things your parents teach you, experiences you have, things you learn at church, things you learn from the Bible.

Learn them well — plan ahead for your future!

Remember:
A Super Hero ... plans ahead.

51

Part of the Team

Two can stand back-to-back and conquer.
Three are even better, for a triple-braided
cord is not easily broken.

— ECCLESIASTES 4:12 —

You don't have to make it through life by yourself. It's God's plan for people to work together. Your family and friends help you, encourage you and teach you.

Working together with other people who serve God means a lot more of God's work will get done. More people will learn to love Him and others. A team of people help each other live for God!

Remember:
A Super Hero ... is a team player.

A New Direction

God commands everyone everywhere to
repent of their sins and turn to Him.

— ACTS 17:30 —

OK, so maybe repent isn't a word you use a lot. What does it mean? It means to turn away from something that you were doing.

When you repent from sin, you turn away from the wrong thing you were doing. Yep, just turn your back on it and head in a new direction — a direction of obeying God.

Repenting is not always easy. But, God will help you be strong if you ask Him.

Remember:

A Super Hero ... repents.

Caring for Others

If I had such faith that I could move mountains,
but didn't love others, I would be nothing.
— 1 CORINTHIANS 13:2 —

Some guys don't care at all about other people. They want everyone to pay attention to them. They don't care about anyone else's problems. They don't care if someone is sad. They just care about themselves.

A Super Hero cares about others. He wants to help others. He cheers for them. He celebrates with them when they win. He doesn't think he is more important than anyone else.

Remember:

A Super Hero ... pays attention to others.

God Is Waiting

The LORD must wait for you to come to Him so He can show you His love and compassion. For the LORD is a faithful God. Blessed are those who wait for His help.

— ISAIAH 30:18 —

Remember:
A Super Hero ...
asks God for help.

You know you should obey God.
You know you should obey your parents.
You know you should respect your teachers.

You want to do what's right, but
sometimes you don't. What can you do?

Ask God's help. He wants you to
ask. He doesn't push into your life.
He's waiting for you to ask!

55

Learning Patience

Be strengthened with all God's glorious power so you
will have all the endurance and patience you need.
— COLOSSIANS 1:11 —

Waiting for your birthday or for Christmas takes forever!
Waiting to be old enough to do certain things is hard.
Waiting takes patience, and patience must be learned.

How do you learn patience? Ask God to help you
think about something else. Find something to
keep busy. Help your parents, play with your
brother or sister. Pretty soon you'll discover
you have learned patience.

Remember:
A Super Hero ... learns patience.

Taking Care of Yourself

Your body is the temple of the Holy Spirit, who lives in you and was given to you by God. You do not belong to yourself.
— 1 CORINTHIANS 6:19 —

Your body is a gift from God. So, brushing your teeth, taking a shower, eating healthy food, getting enough rest, getting exercise ... all of these things are important for you to stay healthy and take care of the body He gave you.

Taking good care of your body shows God how thankful you are to have it!

Remember:
A Super Hero ... takes care of himself.

57

Saying Sorry

The Holy Spirit produces this kind of fruit in our lives: love, joy, peace, patience, kindness, goodness, faithfulness, gentleness, and self-control.

— GALATIANS 5:22-23 —

A Super Hero says he is sorry if he hurts someone. Saying sorry is hard to say, but it makes a big difference.

God says we are to love other people and to live in peace with them. To do that, you must be willing to say, "I know I messed up. I'm sorry."

You're a Super Hero. Do you say, "I'm sorry"?

Remember:
A Super Hero ... says he is sorry.

The Honor of Knowing God

> Cling to your faith in Christ,
> and keep your conscience clear.
> — 1 TIMOTHY 1:19 —

Have you gone to Sunday school and church ever since you were born? Maybe your parents read you stories from the Bible and pray with you every night at bedtime. They are teaching you about faith in God.

Faith in God is serious. He made it possible for you to know Him by sending Jesus to die for your sins.

A Super Hero takes his faith seriously and learns as much about God as he can.

Remember:
A Super Hero ... takes faith seriously.

Noticing Lonely People

"Love each other in the same way I have loved you."
— JOHN 15:12 —

Do you have friends? Do you have a great family? It's cool to have friends and family you enjoy being with.

Do you know anyone who doesn't have any friends? Someone who just moved to town? Or a guy who is a little different? Do you think they might be lonely? If you would be a friend to him, maybe others would be his friend too.

A Super Hero is a friend to those who are lonely.

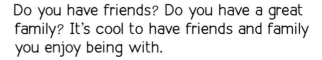

Remember:
A Super Hero ... is a friend to the lonely.

It's a Big World

"You will be My witnesses,
telling people about Me everywhere."
— ACTS 1:8 —

Remember:
A Super Hero ...
thinks about
people around
the world.

There is a whole world outside of your town, your state and even your country. A Super Hero remembers that there are people around the world who haven't yet heard about Jesus. There are people who need homes and food.

What does a Super Hero do about that? He prays for people around the world. He gives money so that missionaries can tell people about Jesus and help them have homes and food. You CAN make a difference in your own small way, which pleases Jesus.

Everyday Blessings

Let us come to Him with thanksgiving. Let us sing psalms of praise to Him!
— PSALM 95:2 —

What does it mean to worship God daily? It means that every day you notice something awesome that God made, and you TELL Him that you noticed. Thank Him for the beautiful world He made. Thank Him for your home, your family and your friends.

Worshiping God means believing that He loves you so much that He would do anything for you ... and He does everything for you every day!

Remember:
A Super Hero ... worships God daily.

Deep-Down Happiness

Always be full of joy in the Lord. I say it again – rejoice!
— PHILIPPIANS 4:4 —

Do you know anyone who is a Grumpy Gus? Someone who is hard to get along with? This kind of person sees the bad in everything and not the good. This person has no joy in his life.

Happiness and joy are not the same. Happiness comes and goes, depending on what is going on. Joy comes from deep inside, because you know that God loves you and takes care of you.

Remember:
A Super Hero ... is full of joy.

63 Shaking off Disappointment

> We can rejoice, too, when we run into problems and trials,
> for we know that they help us develop endurance.
>
> — ROMANS 5:3 —

How do you behave when you are disappointed? Temper tantrum? Pout for a while?

A Super Hero understands that sometimes you don't get what you want. Sometimes you must wait for things. It's OK to be disappointed for a little bit, but then it's best to turn your attention to something else and not keep thinking about your disappointment. That's how a Super Hero handles disappointment.

Remember:
A Super Hero ... handles disappointment.

A Big, Giant THANK YOU!

> Devote yourselves to prayer with an
> alert mind and a thankful heart.
>
> — COLOSSIANS 4:2 —

"YAY, GOD!!!" That's what God deserves when He answers your prayers, right? When He hears you pray for something ... and then He answers, you need to celebrate!

You celebrate when good things happen, right? Well, what could be better than God hearing your prayer and giving you what you asked? That deserves even more than a simple "Thanks." It deserves a giant "THANK YOU! WAY TO GO, GOD!"

Remember:
A Super Hero ... celebrates answered prayer.

What's Most Important?

Honesty guides good people; dishonesty destroys treacherous people.
— PROVERBS 11:3 —

Whew. This is hard. Everyone likes to win. Sometimes you may be tempted to cheat a little bit just to make sure you win.

But, God's Super Hero doesn't do that. He plays by the rules. He plays fair. If he wins, he celebrates. If he loses, he congratulates the winner.

No, it isn't always easy to do this. But, it is the right thing to do. In God's eyes, playing fair is more important than winning.

Remember:
A Super Hero ... plays by the rules.

A Real Super Hero

Be humble, thinking of others as better than yourselves.
— PHILIPPIANS 2:3 —

Remember:
A Super Hero ...
doesn't hurt
others.

You've watched Super Heroes beat bad guys and rescue good guys, right? That's what Super Heroes do. But, as a Super Hero, you must keep in mind that you can't hurt others. You can't beat them up. You can't hurt their feelings. You can't cheat them or make them feel bad.

God's Super Hero doesn't do any of those things. It might seem fun or a good idea at the time, but you will regret it later. God's Super Hero plays nice, cares about others and, most of all, cares about obeying God!

Accepting God's Forgiveness

"Though your sins are like scarlet, I will make them as white as snow."
— ISAIAH 1:18 —

You know that you mess up sometimes. You make mistakes. You hurt others. You do things that God says you shouldn't do.

What do you do then? You tell God that you're sorry and that you won't do those things again. You ask Him to forgive you and you know what? He does! Then, you just need to believe that He has forgiven you and that you can start fresh. Isn't that awesome?

Remember:
A Super Hero ... accepts God's forgiveness.

Helping a Friend

"Now I am giving you a new commandment: Love each other.
Just as I have loved you, you should love each other."

— JOHN 13:34 —

A Super Hero pays attention to a friend who is having a hard time. When your friend has a problem, you don't just say, "Oh well," and walk away.

No, a Super Hero finds a way to encourage his friend by listening to him. By doing things with him. By reminding him that God loves him. By ... being a friend.

Remember:
A Super Hero ... encourages a friend.

69

Believing God's Word

"I am going to prepare a place for you. When everything is ready, I will come and get you, so that you will always be with Me where I am."

— JOHN 14:2-3 —

What about oxygen, or electricity? You can't see these things, but you know they are real, don't you? Is it hard to believe something is real if you can't see it or touch it?

You can believe that heaven is real, because the Bible says it is. Jesus said that He was going to get it ready for you to live there someday. It takes faith to believe it's real.

Remember:
A Super Hero ... knows heaven is real.

Hard Work Won't Hurt You

> Work willingly at whatever you do, as though you were working for the Lord rather than for people.
>
> — COLOSSIANS 3:23 —

Work is ... work. Sometimes work is hard. Different things are hard for different people. Some people have to work hard to learn to read. Some have to work hard to learn math. Some struggle with sports.

A Super Hero works hard, because it's good to learn new things. It's good to work hard to make whatever abilities God gave you the best they can be.

Remember:
A Super Hero ... is willing to work hard.

No Resentment

To learn, you must love discipline; it is stupid to hate correction.
— PROVERBS 12:1 —

It's not fun to be criticized. But, when someone corrects you to help you learn how to do something better, then that's a good thing.

So, don't get crabby and pouty when you are corrected. Try to have the attitude of, "Thanks. I'll try to do things the way you are suggesting. Thank you for taking the time to teach me."

A Super Hero learns from correction instead of resenting it.

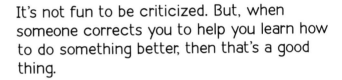

Remember:
A Super Hero ... accepts correction with a good attitude.

Turning the Other Cheek

You must all be quick to listen,
slow to speak, and slow to get angry.
— JAMES 1:19 —

Remember:
A Super Hero ...
stops fights.

It's not easy to be nice when someone is mean to you. But you know what happens if you're mean back? A fight starts. Nothing good ever comes from reacting like this.

God's Super Hero doesn't let that happen. He tries to stop the fight by being kind to someone who is being mean. Or ... he walks away and lets the other guy cool down.

Do what you can to stop fights – not make them bigger!

Following the Leader?

How can a young person stay pure? By obeying the LORD's word.
— PSALM 119:9 —

Sometimes there is one guy in a group of friends who is kind of the leader. He is usually a lot of fun and he comes up with ideas of things to do. Some guys just go along with what he suggests.

If you're one of the guys who follows the leader, you need to be careful. Why? Just be careful that the guy you follow does not lead you away from obeying God.

Remember:
A Super Hero ... is careful whom he follows.

As Good as Your Word

The godly are directed by honesty; the wicked fall beneath their load of sin.
— PROVERBS 11:5 —

Your promise is your word. Keeping your word shows that you are a person who can be trusted. If you make promises, but don't keep them, then people will stop trusting you.

Here are some tips to be a Super Hero of your word: Don't make promises you can't keep and think before you make a promise.

When you make a promise, do what you said you would do. That shows that you are a guy who can be trusted.

Remember:
A Super Hero ... keeps his promises.

75

Your Job

Those who have been born into God's family
do not make a practice of sinning,
because God's life is in them.

— 1 JOHN 3:9 —

Jesus died to pay for your sins. He loves you that much. When you asked Jesus into your heart, He forgave your sins. But ... you kept on sinning.

It's your job to break sinful habits like lying, losing your temper, cheating and saying mean things. Ask God for help and strength, but also watch your choices. Choose not to sin. Obeying God is what a Super Hero chooses to do. You can make a fresh start today!

Remember:
A Super Hero ... tries to break sinful habits.

Learning from Problems

> If you need wisdom, ask our generous God, and He will give it to you. He will not rebuke you for asking.
>
> — JAMES 1:5 —

No one likes to have troubles. It's hard to see anything good that can come from having troubles.

Look at your problems like a lesson that you have to learn. When you have a problem, ask God to show you what you can learn from it.

If you learn a lesson, then you may not have that problem ever again!

Remember:
A Super Hero ... learns from his problems.

Trusting God Always

God is our refuge and strength,
always ready to help in times of trouble.
— PSALM 46:1 —

When bad things happen, do you wonder where God is? Do you wonder if He is paying attention? When you pray really hard about something but nothing changes, do you want to give up?

A Super Hero doesn't give up on God. Even when he doesn't understand what's going on, he believes God is in control. He trusts God – no matter what – even in the hard times!

Remember:
A Super Hero ... stays true to God even in hard times.

The Biggest Dreams!

The **LORD** your God is living among you. He is a
Mighty Savior. He will take delight in you with gladness.
— ZEPHANIAH 3:17 —

Remember:
A Super Hero ...
dreams big.

What do you want to be when you grow up? Do you have dreams of doing something amazing? What's your dream? Becoming a fireman? A doctor? A mountain climber? A vet?

You never know what God has planned for you. Maybe by dreaming big He will be able to direct your steps into exactly what He wants you to do!

Dream big, because God is even bigger than your dreams!

Learning from the Wise Ones

Fools think their own way is right, but the wise listen to others.
— PROVERBS 12:15 —

A Super Hero knows that some people know more than he does. They know more because they are older and have had more experiences. Or maybe they know a lot because they have studied or because they have known God longer.

These people can give you good advice. So, a Super Hero listens to what they tell him and he learns from them.

Learn from those who have things to teach you.

Remember:
A Super Hero ... listens to wise advice.

Calm Down

A fool is quick-tempered, but a wise person stays calm when insulted.
— PROVERBS 12:16 —

Be careful when you get mad. You may say things you don't mean. You might do things that hurt others. Slow down and think about what you say and what you do.

Things said and done in anger can really hurt other people. It's hard to take back words and actions that hurt others.

A Super Hero asks God to help him control his anger so that his love for God always shines through.

Remember:
A Super Hero ... is careful when he's angry.

81

Take It to God

Give all your worries and cares to God,
for He cares about you.

— 1 PETER 5:7 —

Are you scared sometimes? Do you worry about stuff all the time? Don't allow fear and worry to control you. This is not how God wants you to live.

The best thing to do when you're scared or worried is to tell God about it. Ask Him to help you get over being scared. Ask him to take care of you. He will. In His time and in His way.

Remember:
A Super Hero ... takes his worries to God.

Let People Be

> Above all, clothe yourselves with love, which
> binds us all together in perfect harmony.
> — COLOSSIANS 3:14 —

Wouldn't it be boring if all people were just the same? It's a good thing that people are all different. But sometimes those differences become things we don't like about each other.

God's Super Hero knows it's OK for his buddies to like different things and just be different. He doesn't judge them. That's not his job. God is the only judge! The most important thing to do is to love one another.

Remember:
A Super Hero ... doesn't judge others.

83

A New Day

Nothing can ever separate us from God's love.
— ROMANS 8:38 —

Did you ever have one of those days where everything goes wrong? A day when it feels like every choice you make is the wrong one and then you are constantly in trouble? Not fun.

Thankfully, every day is a fresh start. A chance to be kind to others. A chance to obey your parents. A chance to show God that you're serious about loving Him and others. Fresh starts are a good thing.

Remember:
A Super Hero ... is thankful for fresh starts.

A Job Well Done

Those who trust in the LORD will find new strength.
They will soar high on wings like eagles. They will run
and not grow weary. They will walk and not faint.
— ISAIAH 40:31 —

Remember:
A Super Hero ...
finishes what he
starts.

If you're cleaning your room ... do you finish
the whole room or clean only part of
it and then stop tidying up and start
playing?

God's Super Hero finishes his work,
whatever it is. A job isn't well done
until it's all done. Ask God to help
you finish what you start.

You will feel much better if you
first finish your chores. Then it'll
be time for fun.

Forgiving Yourself

Who dares accuse us whom God has chosen for His own? No one -
for God Himself has given us right standing with Himself.
— ROMANS 8:33 —

God forgives you. When you sin and tell Him you're sorry and ask Him to forgive you ... He does and never mentions it again. How cool is that?

Sometimes the harder thing is to forgive yourself. Don't keep thinking about how you messed up. That keeps you from a fresh start. Let go of your guilt — forgive yourself. God did!

Remember:
A Super Hero ... lets go of guilt.

Caring for People

He comforts us in all our troubles so that we can comfort others. When they are troubled, we will be able to give them the same comfort God has given us.

— 2 CORINTHIANS 1:4 —

It's hard to know what to say when a friend is sad. Sometimes it is easier to not say anything.

You don't have to have the perfect words to say. Your friend will feel better just to hear you say, "I'm sorry you're sad." Let people know you care.

Remember:
A Super Hero ... comforts people who are sad.

87

Noticing Your Blessings

Give thanks to the LORD and proclaim His greatness.
Let the whole world know what He has done.
— 1 CHRONICLES 16:8 —

Stop and think about your life for a minute – your home, your family, your friends. Do you have a pretty good life? A home to live in? Food every day? A good school? Those things are called blessings. They are all gifts to you from God.

In fact, everything you have is a blessing from God. It's a good idea to stop once in a while and notice how many blessings God has given you. Then, thank Him.

Remember:
A Super Hero ... counts his blessings.

Thanking God for Your Family

> Be thankful in all circumstances, for this is God's will for you who belong to Christ Jesus.
> — 1 THESSALONIANS 5:18 —

Families are great. Sure, you may have trouble obeying your parents once in a while. But your family will love you ... no matter what. They take care of you. They watch out for you. They help you become the best "you" that you can be.

Thank God for your family and ask Him to take care of each of them and bless them every day. Remember, God placed you in your family so you wouldn't be alone. He expects you to love them and care for them.

Remember:
A Super Hero ... is thankful for his family.

Our Wonderful World

The LORD is the everlasting God, the Creator of all the earth.
— ISAIAH 40:28 —

God made gigantic mountains that are so high their tops are covered by clouds. God made oceans so deep that the bottom is seldom seen. God made tiny flowers and big trees to shade our yards. God made waterfalls, rivers, fields of flowers, forests ... well, God made it all.

Praise God for all He has made. Thank Him for it all. Enjoy creation and take care of it for Him!

Remember:
A Super Hero ... praises God for His creation.

Daily Habits

Three things will last forever – faith, hope, and love – and the greatest of these is love.
— 1 CORINTHIANS 13:13 —

When you do something over and over, it becomes a habit. The best thing to do is to make good habits. It might be hard at first, but you'll find it easier to do every day.

Things you do every day, like making time to pray and making time to read your Bible, are good habits.

Make it a habit to be kind and respectful to others. What other good habits can you make?

Here Lies a Dead Lie

Stop telling lies. Let us tell our neighbors the truth,
for we are all parts of the same body.
— EPHESIANS 4:25 —

Lies are untrue things said about other people. Lies are untrue things about yourself (like how you scored a bazillion points on a video game when you didn't really).

NO kind of lie is OK. Maybe you don't START lies. But, if you pass them on, you're just as guilty as the person who started them. Let lies die with you — don't pass them on!

Remember:
A Super Hero ... doesn't spread lies.

Let It Go

"Even if that person wrongs you seven times a day and each time turns again and asks forgiveness, you must forgive."
— LUKE 17:4 —

Everyone gets mad once in a while. How you deal with anger is what matters. Do you keep thinking about whatever it was that made you angry? Do you think about getting even with the person responsible?

That's called "feeding your anger" and it only makes things worse ... for you. Let it go. Forgive and forget. Your mind and heart will be healthier.

Remember:
A Super Hero ... lets go of anger.

God Cares

Give your burdens to the LORD, and He will take care of you. He will not permit the godly to slip and fall.
— PSALM 55:22 —

God cares when you are sad, lonely, angry or happy. God cares because He loves you. So, when you need to be comforted, go to God and tell Him how you are feeling. He is available 24/7 and is waiting to hear from you.

Read His Word and let the messages of His love make you feel better.

Think about God's love and care and let that comfort your heart and make you feel better.

Remember:
A Super Hero ... accepts God's comfort.

Taking Responsibility

> I confess my sins; I am deeply sorry for what I have done.
> — PSALM 38:18 —

You can try to never do anything wrong. But, all people are sinners who are trying to learn how to obey God and live for Him. But it's important that when you do sin, you admit it.

Don't make excuses about how it is someone else's fault or that you were tired or mad. Just admit it. Tell God you're sorry and ask Him to help you do better. He will.

Remember:
A Super Hero ... does not depend on excuses.

Your Choices

"Anyone who listens to My teaching and follows it is wise,
like a person who builds a house on solid rock."
— MATTHEW 7:24 —

It's easier to follow Jesus when you are around others who follow Him. But there will be times when you are with friends who do not follow Jesus. Then it will up to you to CHOOSE to obey Him — no matter what.

Your choice to do that will be a good example to others of who God is and how much He loves them too.

Remember:
A Super Hero ... follows Jesus, no matter what.

Giving Your Best

96

Never be lazy, but work hard and serve the Lord enthusiastically.
— ROMANS 12:11 —

Remember:
A Super Hero ... gives his best to God.

Does doing your "best" mean that you never make mistakes? No, it doesn't. It means that your attitude is to try your hardest and to do the best you can do.

Sometimes you will do better than other times. But if, in your heart, you want to give God your best performance, best obedience, best devotion ... well, that's all He asks for. If you want to give your best, then you will.

Taking Sin Seriously

Humble yourselves before God. Resist the devil, and he will flee from you.
— JAMES 4:7 —

Are there "BIG" sins and "little" sins? If you think so, then you might think that the sins you do are just little sins and not such a big deal. After all, you don't murder or rob banks, right?

Well, sin is sin. If you do things that disobey God's Word, it's sin. Don't take sin lightly. Tell God you are sorry (and mean it).

Remember:
A Super Hero ... doesn't take sin lightly.

What Makes a Good Friend?

Love is patient and kind. Love is not jealous or boastful or proud or rude. It does not demand its own way. It is not irritable, and it keeps no record of being wronged.
— 1 CORINTHIANS 13:4-5 —

How do you want your friends to treat you?
You want them to play fair.
You want them to be kind.
You want them to be honest.
You want them to stand up for you.

What else can you add? Those are things that you should do to be a good friend.

Remember:
A Super Hero ... is a loyal friend.

An Argument Stopper

> "If someone slaps you on the right cheek, offer the other cheek also."
> — MATTHEW 5:39 —

Some people just like to argue. It's almost like a game to them. But when an argument starts, it usually ends with someone's feelings (or body) being hurt.

God's Super Hero will try to stop arguments instead of making them bigger. There are peaceful ways to settle differences and those are the best ways.

Take care of your friendships and help your friends ... stop arguments instead of feeding them!

Remember:
A Super Hero ... tries to stop arguments.

Taking Turns

Always be humble and gentle. Be patient with each other, making allowance for each other's faults.

— EPHESIANS 4:2 —

Do you take turns with your friends or do you always have to be the one in charge? God's Super Hero gives others a chance to be the boss once in a while. He doesn't always need to get his own way.

Sometimes you will get to play your favorite game and sometimes you'll play your friends' favorite things. That's fair and kind. Be a good sport and make sure that you and your friends take turns. It's the God-thing to do!

Remember:
A Super Hero ... does not always have to be the boss.

Trust Brings Courage

You will keep in perfect peace all who trust in You,
all whose thoughts are fixed on You!
— ISAIAH 26:3 —

You don't really know yet how much courage you're going to need in life. But, if you start the habit right now of asking God to give you courage for whatever happens, your trust in Him will grow stronger.

Then, when you get older and things happen where you need more courage, you will automatically turn to God. Your courage will come from your trust in Him!

Remember:
A Super Hero ... gets his courage from God.